S0-ARH-862

1959 op
4⁵⁰

WEEKLY READER
Children's Book Club
Education Center • Columbus 16, Ohio

PRESENTS

WONDERS OF THE DEEP SEA
and
WONDERS OF THE OCEAN ZOO

By BORIS ARNOV, JR.
and HELEN MATHER-SMITH MINDLIN

Wonders of the
DEEP SEA

by BORIS ARNOV, JR., and
HELEN MATHER-SMITH MINDLIN

ILLUSTRATED BY CHARLES MATHER-SMITH

DODD, MEAD & COMPANY • NEW YORK

WEEKLY READER
Children's Book Club
Edition, 1961

© 1959 by Boris Arnov, Jr., and Helen Mather-Smith Mindlin
All rights reserved
No part of this book may be reproduced in any form
without permission in writing from the publisher.

Library of Congress Catalog Card Number: 59-7992
Printed in the United States of America

American Book-Stratford Press, Inc., New York

TO ALL THOSE WHO LOVE THE SEA

CONTENTS

I
HOW THE
OCEANS BEGAN

The Story in Rocks

Billions of years ago, when our earth was formed, there were neither oceans nor land, and life did not yet exist. Most scientists believe that our earth originally exploded away from the huge sun mass and went whizzing off into the sky.

If you had been there to witness the birth of the world, you would probably have seen an awesome sight! Scientists tell us that our earth was first a red hot ball of melted rock and there were terrific explosions which sent hissing clouds of steam rocketing into the skies — and all this while the new planet was spinning like a top.

It took thousands of years for the earth to cool down and during this time, the steam rising from it formed huge clouds that blotted out the sun, keeping everything in total darkness. When this gigantic ball of fire cooled, it did not become smooth like a marble. Instead, it wrinkled up like a dried prune, forming folds and hollows. The high parts of the wrinkles became the continents and the places in between the wrinkles were the hollowed out beds for the oceans.

Some scientists think that the water in the oceans came from deep inside the cooling earth, but others believe that the massive clouds surrounding our new-born planet became so heavy that they poured down flooding rains. These rains were not just downpours as we know them now, but the water must have come in a solid deluge, with flashing lightning and thunderstorms that lasted for thousands of years. Finally, large bodies of water lay on our earth, gathered in the folds of its wrinkled crust. These were the first oceans.

But this did not last. Later on, for unknown reasons, the air surrounding the earth became cool and tremendous quantities of ice formed on the new planet. Enormous expanses of sea water were frozen into great glaciers and the oceans fell lower and lower until dry land emerged once more. Then, when warmer weather returned, most of the ice melted and again the oceans began to rise. This ice melted and froze several times throughout the millions of years which this process took.

Even right now, our planet is going through changes — one of these being the gradual rising of the oceans. This is due to many things, but probably more than any other it is because we are now living during an extremely warm period, when higher temperatures are gradually melting the ice deposits of the world into the oceans.

How are all these things known, you might ask? Through the findings of scientists, studying rock formations which cover the earth in layers of sandstone, slate or limestone. These rocks are very similar to books, telling us many things that happened in the past — how wind, rain and water have worn away high mountains and how low places have filled with earth. Some of these rock books are imprinted with leaves, trees and the skeletons of animals that lived millions of years ago and in this way, the dim past has written part of its story for us.

11

Islands Are Born

In the beginning, the positions of the new oceans were very different from what they are now. Layers of earth, cooling deep down, caused the outer crust sometimes to push up and sometimes to pull down. It seemed as if a giant hand were changing the earth's surface — almost as you do at the seashore when you make a sand-hill. The water rushed in where holes and canyons were formed and flowed away where mountains pushed up, causing shore lines to change and new continents to rise up from the sea. If there had been people living on earth in those days, they could have walked across where the Gulf of Mexico is now located without even getting their feet wet, for it was all dry land.

Violent earthquakes shook our planet and many volcanoes erupted, popping out of the oceans, rising up to become towering island mountains. Other volcanoes blew themselves to pieces, disappearing entirely and leaving only the calm sea once more.

In some places on our earth, volcanoes are still doing their part to build more land or change the earth's face, still erupting and pouring out the melted rock called lava. One of these — the island of Krakatoa, which was located between Sumatra and Java — erupted in 1883, exploding with the noise of an atom bomb. It was heard thousands of miles away and it caused a wave of water eighty feet high. This great wave flooded nearby islands, capsized big ships at sea and caused the death of over thirty-six thousand people. Another volcano, called Mount Pelee, located on the island of Martinique, erupted in 1902, killing thirty thousand people. Even now, there are active volcanoes in the South Pacific, Hawaii and the Azore Islands.

There was once no water in the Gulf of Mexico.

When our earth first formed, some volcanoes, instead of blowing themselves to pieces, remained as rugged lava islands. Others of the volcanic islands gradually sank into the sea and all trace of these would be lost if it were not for a strange growth called coral — little animals that build hard limestone skeleton houses around themselves.

These coral animals often gathered in a ring around the volcanic island. When the volcano had sunk, all that was left was the circle of coral, enclosing a deep lagoon. These coral formations came to be known as atolls.

An atoll looks like a big doughnut in the middle of the ocean and the coral animals keep building on to it, making it larger all the time with their limestone skeletons. After many years, pieces of this coral, along with floating debris which has collected in the lagoon, fills the atoll. Eventually, it is no longer shaped like a doughnut but, instead, begins to look like an island.

An atoll looks like a big doughnut in the middle of the ocean.

There are many kinds of coral in the sea.

The barren little island gradually collects bits of weeds, wood, plants and other things floating around in the ocean and, after many more years, soil is built up from all these odds and ends. Then seeds from plants that once grew faraway are washed ashore and take root. The desolate place becomes larger and greener and soon it looks just like the pictures we all have seen of beautiful tropical islands.

Although our earth had already been formed, there were still no people or animals living on it when the oceans began to fill with life. First there were tiny sea animals that were very different from any kind we know of now. Then there came odd-appearing fishes, gigantic reptiles and creatures that looked like nightmares. We can really only guess at many of these strange happenings of our earth and its oceans for they are still like an unsolved mystery story. Scientists are constantly at work, trying to unravel these problems, just like detectives following clues. Perhaps sometime we will discover the fascinating answers to questions that puzzle us today.

II
WHAT
THE OCEAN IS

The Seven Seas

When you know the ocean only from visiting or even living at the seashore, it is difficult to get an idea of the enormous size of the body of water in which you play and go swimming. But if you are ever lucky enough to take a voyage on a large ship, you will find out that you can sail for days and cross thousands of miles of water before sighting land. Then, you might be able to realize how big an ocean really can be and that much more sea water covers our earth than land.

Although all water is made up mainly of hydrogen and oxygen, the oceans contain many other substances besides. These are called elements and they are found in some form in all matter. Sea water has more than ninety of these elements, among which are sulphur, aluminum, iodine, iron, copper and even gold and silver.

In order to help us locate the oceans of the world, they have been marked off on the accompanying map as the Atlantic, Pacific and Indian Oceans. The Arctic Ocean, which is really part of the

Atlantic, and the Antarctic, which is on the other side of our earth, have no true boundaries of their own. All five of these oceans are thousands of miles long and wide but the Pacific is by far the largest. It stretches for almost seventy million square miles — an area much greater than that of all the continents of the world combined.

Some few people still divide these great masses of sea water on our planet into "seven seas," just as the old-time sailors used to do. They divide both the Atlantic and Pacific Oceans into two parts, calling those areas above the equator the North Atlantic and North Pacific and the parts below the equator the South Atlantic and South Pacific, then the Indian, Arctic and Antarctic bodies of water make seven oceans in all, according to their calculations. However, this idea is not the generally accepted one today.

There are other large bodies of water called seas. These are really extensions of the oceans, being separated from them by projections from the mainland or islands. For example, the Bering Sea, between Alaska and Russia; the Mediterranean Sea, which separates Europe from Africa; and the Caribbean Sea, where the islands of the West Indies are located.

Other portions of the ocean that extend far into the land are called gulfs — such as the Gulf of Mexico and the Gulf of California. Smaller bodies of water similar to these are called bays.

The oceans and other bodies of water are usually light green or muddy colored in shallow places and blue, gray or dark green in the deep parts, depending upon the reflections from the sky. This changes color according to whether it is a sunny or cloudy day at the time that you are looking. But some bodies of water have been given unusual names because they are colored by animal life and plants living in their depths or because muddy rivers flow into them. The Red Sea and the Yellow Sea are examples of this.

These oceans, gulfs and bays may be calm or rough, shallow or deep, but all of them together form millions of square miles and billions of tons of water, and most of them touch lands strange to us where the language and customs of the people are different from our own.

ASIA

NORT

AM

Pacific

Ocean

Indian
Ocean AUSTRALIA

20

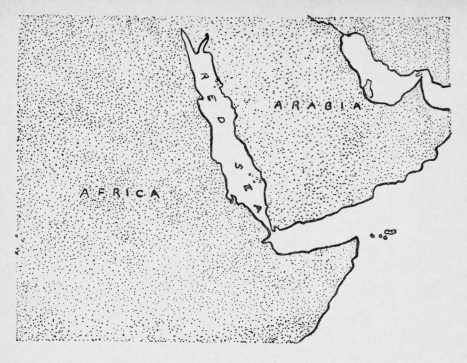

Why the Ocean is Salty

By now you are probably wondering, "How did the oceans get to be so salty?"

Many scientists believe that they have the correct answer by explaining that, after our world was formed and after it had rained for centuries, salty mineral rock was gradually dissolved by the rain and spring-fed rivers and this salt was carried down to the oceans. When we remember that this happened for thousands of years, it is not so hard to understand how the oceans became so salty.

There is enough salt in all the oceans to build a mountain higher than any now on earth. Some seas are saltier than others and the Red Sea, which lies between the hot deserts of Arabia and Africa, is the saltiest of all. If you were to swim in it, you would find it difficult to sink or to dive to the bottom. The reason for this is that the more salt there is in water, the more weight it can hold up.

You may want to try a simple experiment and see for yourself how this works. Fill a bowl with fresh water and place an egg in its shell in it. The egg will immediately sink to the bottom. But if you

There is enough salt in all the oceans to build a mountain higher than any now on earth.

keep adding salt to the water, the egg will finally float and you will have your own miniature salty sea.

The more salt there is in water, the more weight it can hold up.

III
HOW
THE OCEAN ACTS

Rivers in the Ocean

Perhaps the most remarkable thing about oceans all over the world is their great rivers. It might seem very odd to you, but in the oceans there are mighty rivers, flowing along on courses that have remained much the same for thousands of years — rivers that have no rocky banks or sandy shores to guide them as do those on land.

These rivers running through the oceans are not small streams. Instead, some are so large that they make the world's widest and longest land rivers, such as the Nile, Amazon and Mississippi, seem like small streams in comparison!

The faster ocean rivers move along at five miles an hour — just about as fast as you can walk — and these are called currents or streams. The slower rivers that flow through the oceans are called drifts or creeps.

Let us look at the area on the map where, way down between Cuba and Yucatan, it is so warm all the time that there is no winter and you can swim in the ocean any day of the year. It is here that the most famous ocean river, the Gulf Stream, begins after having flowed along from waters near South America.

The Gulf Stream

27

The prevailing winds in this area, called the trade winds, push this warmed tropical water toward the west. As the current flows, it gradually bends from the equator toward the north. This is caused by the earth revolving on its axis. Taking a direction toward the northwest, the main branch follows its course through the Gulf of Mexico, until it comes rushing out through the narrow straits between Florida and Cuba into the Atlantic Ocean.

This great ocean river continues on a course northward, following the eastern coast line of the United States, but gradually it veers farther eastward. As the Gulf Stream dips close to the shores of the United States, especially near Florida, it sends warmed air over the land. Each minute of the day, almost two billion tons of Gulf Stream water flow along the Florida coast, often reaching a half mile deep and forty miles wide. Later, off Nova Scotia, this ocean river spreads out to the enormous width of two hundred and fifty miles.

It is not difficult for a boat captain to tell when he is in this great current, for the waters of the Gulf Stream are a deep, indigo blue, and warmer than the surrounding waters. Besides this, the Gulf Stream flows fast enough through the ocean so that ripples are often seen along its edges. Also, when it passes through cool regions, its warm waters may steam as its surface area is chilled by the cold air above it.

By now you are probably wondering how the Gulf Stream was discovered in all the thousands of miles of open ocean. It came about in an odd way. For many years, some of the old-time sea captains kept the Gulf Stream a dark secret from others. They would use this steadily flowing ocean river to push them along faster as they traveled on a northward course. People could not figure out why certain ships delivered their cargo sooner than others sailing for the same port. Finally, Benjamin Franklin found out about this fast moving current from a captain friend and he made a map, showing its approximate course. The secret was out! From that time on, all charts showed this ocean river. Ships sailing northward in the Atlantic Ocean, near the United States, used the Gulf Stream to propel them more rapidly, while those going southward tried to avoid its strong current as much as possible.

As the Gulf Stream continues north along the eastern coast of the United States, it takes a slight turn around the Carolinas and heads to the northeast. Soon it comes in contact with the waters of another great ocean river called the Labrador Current. For the most part, each current travels its own route. The Gulf Stream continues on a course across the Atlantic Ocean, sending off branches to several areas on its way. These smaller currents warm the coasts of the British Isles, Iceland, Norway, Sweden, Denmark and other countries on the North Sea.

The people who live in the cold countries much nearer to the North Pole than we do are mighty lucky to have the Gulf Stream flowing nearby, for it has been said that, if it were not for this wonderful, warm current, these areas would probably be bleak, ice-covered lands, with snowbanks that never melted.

The Gulf Stream is so reliable in the direction in which it flows that if you should toss a bottle with a message inside into this current and the bottle had an uninterrupted journey, it would probably arrive in one of the countries bordering on the North Sea in about eight or ten weeks. It would be almost like a mail carrier that you could depend upon to make regular deliveries from one Gulf Stream post office to another.

The steady flow of the Gulf Stream might even be used to carry a message inside a bottle.

There are other rivers in the ocean nearly as important as the Gulf Stream. The Japanese or Kuroshio Current is one of these. It flows along the coast of Formosa and Japan and is very much like the Gulf Stream in many ways, although not quite so large. This current keeps such places as the Aleutian Islands and Alaska livable and, as it swings around the Pacific Ocean and comes close to the United States, it heats the atmosphere on the West Coast.

For thousands of years, all the creatures in the ocean have taken advantage of these warm ocean rivers and have depended upon them for food. Eggs and larvae of many fishes, tiny plants and animals — which all together are called plankton — start their lives in these huge, heated aquariums. The warm ocean rivers of the world provide food, not only for the floating plankton, but for many other sea creatures which feed upon the plankton. These sea animals, in turn, are eaten by still other large species. The Blue Whale, biggest animal in the world, feeds entirely on the tiny plankton.

Plankton

One of the most unusual things about the ocean is the Sargasso Sea. It lies in the middle of the Atlantic Ocean and is really not a sea at all but rather a large area of water almost as big as the United States. The Gulf Stream flows endlessly around it and there is not much wind to disturb its surface, so enormous beds of floating sargasso weeds gather here.

In the early days, frightened sailors told stories of how you could much wind to disturb its surface, so enormous beds of floating sargasso Sea and about the skeletons of wrecked ships that had been trapped in this weird place. Of course, these stories are not true, for it is known that ships can travel through the Sargasso Sea without any mishap. The lack of wind in this area is the only thing that may prevent the progress of a sailing ship.

Sailors used to believe there were many wrecked ships in the
Sargasso Sea.

Tides

One of the strangest things about the ocean is its tides. Twice each day, for several hours at a time, the water rises, covering sandy or rocky shores and stopping only when "high tide" is reached. Then, slowly, the water level goes down, gradually leaving the sandy shore or rocks dry, until it reaches "low tide." The incoming water is called the "flow" and the outgoing, the "ebb." About every twenty-four hours the ocean ebbs twice and flows twice along most coasts of the world.

If you are drifting in a boat at an inlet — which is a passage where ocean waters enter quiet bays — you will find yourself carried out to sea on the ebb tide without using any oars or a motor. Or, if the tide is flowing, your boat will be floated *into* the bay, as the strong surge of water pushes before it everything that floats.

The unseen force causing these daily tides puzzled men for gen-

erations and some even thought that the earth itself was breathing, so bringing about the rise and fall of the oceans. Not until Isaac Newton explained it to the world was the secret of tides at last understood.

You see, the sun and moon are like enormous magnets, forever pulling at the earth, and this great force makes the tides go higher or lower at certain times. Water moves toward these two large planets just as surely as a plate, slipping from your hands, drops to the floor. This force is known as gravity. Actually, if you could throw a plate high enough into the sky to overcome the pull of the earth's gravity, the plate would be drawn toward the moon, instead of coming back to earth. The oceans, clinging close to our earth, never get far enough away into the skies to be pulled entirely up to any other planets. However, the sun and moon, tugging on the oceans like magnets, are able to draw them a little away from the earth and this is what causes the daily tidal movements.

33

Being closer to our planet, the moon has a greater pulling power than the sun. Sometimes, as the moon travels around the earth, it is closer than at other times, making its pull stronger. Often the sun and moon are pulling from different directions — just like a tug of war in the skies, with the earth in the middle.

Twice each month — during the first sliver of a new moon and, later in the month, when the moon is full — spring tides occur. At these times, the sun and moon are directly in line with the earth, and the two, pulling together cause the tide to rise higher and to ebb lower than at other times during the month.

Also, during each month, when the moon is in its first quarter and later, while it is in its third quarter, there occur neap tides. At this time, the sun, moon and earth form the three points of a triangle in

When the sun, moon and earth are in a straight line, spring tides occur.

the sky. The sun and moon are *not* pulling together. This causes less of a gravitational pull on the earth's oceans and during these times there is less of a difference between high and low tide than at any other time during the month.

If you want to experiment on how the tides work, just take in a deep breath of air and see how your chest expands. When you let out the air, watch your chest go down. This is similar to the way the oceans swell out at flood tide and become lower at ebb tide, as the moon and earth change positions. Wherever there is a great pull on an ocean, causing high tides, another part of the ocean will, at the same time, be in ebb tide. This rhythm goes on continuously, each day having four tides, as we have said — two high and two low — in most parts of the world.

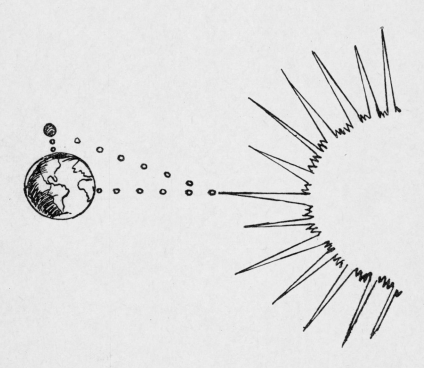

When the sun and moon pull on the earth at right angles to each other, neap tides occur.

Do not expect to find high tides at the same time from one day to the next because each day the moon and sun are in different positions in relation to earth and this has a changing effect on our oceans. As a result, the ebb and flow tides are almost an hour later every day.

Predicting at exactly what time the different tides will occur has become an easy job since the invention of special machines which tell the exact pull of the sun and moon any place in the world. Tide tables are prepared a year or more in advance and you can use them yourself in many interesting ways. If you are a swimmer, you might like to know at what time your favorite beach will have the smallest waves, for these usually occur during the low tides. Or if you want to dig clams, it is a good idea to know when the water will be very low. Fishermen use tide tables to judge when the fish will bite the best, as this is most likely during the time the tide is flowing.

Narrow inlets leading from the ocean to calm, protected waters are often the location of tremendous tidal currents. Places known as narrows or straits — deep, narrow cuts between land — often have tidal currents so strong that many boats must wait to pass through until the tide changes, so that they may go along with the tide and not have to struggle against it.

Tides are different in size in all parts of the world, depending upon the land they touch. On some islands in the middle of the ocean, there is hardly any tidal change at all. In places like the Bay of Fundy, in Nova Scotia, where the tides must pass in and out through the narrow inlet of this funnel-shaped bay, the difference between high and low tide is sixty-two feet.

Strong winds and air pressure may also affect tides. Probably there are many more things influencing tides about which, as yet, we know very little or nothing at all.

In some parts of the world, incoming tides rush through the narrow mouth of a river in a wall of water known as a "bore." These can be very dangerous. The highest tidal bore in the world is the one that pushes up the Tsientang River which empties into the China Sea. During spring tides, this wave of water is sometimes twenty-five feet high and it sweeps in at almost fifteen miles an hour. A boat caught in such a wall of water might be thrown aside like a fragile toy and be destroyed.

The bore that pushes into the Amazon River in South America is not very high but it is far-reaching and can go on up the river for almost two hundred miles before wearing out.

If you ever happen to be near any of these bore waves, it would be a very good idea to get out of the way, for they can indeed be extremely treacherous. A good way to find out *when* these bore waves occur, so you can avoid them, is to study your tide tables.

The highest tidal base in the world is the one that pushes up the Tsientang River.

Life-Giving Currents

Besides the tidal currents in the ocean, there are the great currents such as the Gulf Stream, about which you have already read. Then there are endless flows of criss-crossing lesser currents in all the oceans of the world — some warm and some cold. There are also large expanses of ocean where there is very little current at all.

Did you know that whirlpools come from currents, too? Off the coast of Norway is the most famous whirlpool in the world. It is known as the Maelstrom and sailors once thought that it would swallow big ships, sucking them into its swirling center. Many stories have been written about this well-known whirlpool that spins around at about twelve- to fourteen-miles-an-hour. Even that fine author, Edgar Allan Poe, gave frightening accounts of the dangers in the Maelstrom.

Although it is doubtful that large ships can be sucked down into a whirlpool, it is true that vessels steer clear of them, for they might be caught in the swirling waters, get out of control and smash on nearby rocks.

At Point Wilson, in Puget Sound, there is another treacherous whirlpool and the Inside Passage to Alaska has many of them that must be avoided by ships.

Whirlpools are nothing more than areas of ocean, usually around rocks, where swift currents cause a circular action in the water. It is even possible for you to make your own whirlpool. Just to prove how simple it is, fill a cup with water, then stir it swiftly. Soon the

The Maelstrom

liquid will be forced to the sides of the cup and a hole will form in the very center, just like a real ocean whirlpool.

Other types of currents found in the ocean are those flowing upward and downward in the water. These are called upwellings and downflows. We cannot see them with our eyes but we can detect them with instruments built for the purpose.

These currents are caused by the differences in the temperature of the sea water. Warm water expands and the cold water contracts. Also, cold water is heavier than warm water and it tends to sink, while the lighter warm water rises slowly.

The heavier cold waters coming from the Polar Seas flow along the bottom of the oceans toward the tropics. The warm waters coming from the tropics and heated by the sun spread over the oceans' surface as they flow toward the Polar Seas.

When all this churned up water of the deep oceans either rises or descends, many important things happen. With the upwellings come vast quantities of minerals that mix through the upper layers of water and provide a kind of fertilizer for the plankton. As you know, the plankton is very important in providing food for many of the oceans' larger animals.

The ocean also depends upon downflows to carry from the surface to the depths great quantities of oxygen which stir up the deep areas so that they do not become stagnant. Some places in the Black Sea and the fjords of Norway, for instance, do not have these puri-fying downflows. There is no motion of the bottom water and, as a result, it has become so poisonous that animal life cannot exist in it. When, occasionally, there is such a terrific storm that the deep, poisonous waters come to the surface, thousands of fish are killed.

A very interesting downflow that offers scientists much to study is found in the Strait of Gibraltar, the narrow neck of water connecting the Atlantic Ocean with the Mediterranean Sea. Now the Mediterranean is a warm sea, and the hot rays of the sun cause it to lose water continually by evaporation. This, of course, takes place everywhere in the world but to a particularly great extent in this sea. Thousands of gallons of fresh water are drawn up to the clouds each day. Since the salt in the sea water is too heavy to evaporate, the Mediterranean Sea becomes saltier and saltier. This has been going on for many years, so the Mediterranean is now much saltier than the Atlantic Ocean, which is right next to it.

At the Strait of Gibraltar, the heavier salty water of the Mediterranean flows out into the Atlantic Ocean, sinking close to the bottom. This escape of water causes the level of the Mediterranean Sea to fall and the less salty water from the Atlantic Ocean rushes in to replace it. This in-rushing water stays *above* the level of the outgoing water because it has less salt and so is lighter. Therefore, at Gibraltar, there are two separate currents, one above the other and moving in opposite directions.

In the days when ships had only sails to propel them, this upper flow of water into the Mediterranean was too fast for them to overcome and vessels had to wait to leave the Sea, sometimes for long periods, until strong pushing winds would arise, and they could sail into the Atlantic Ocean.

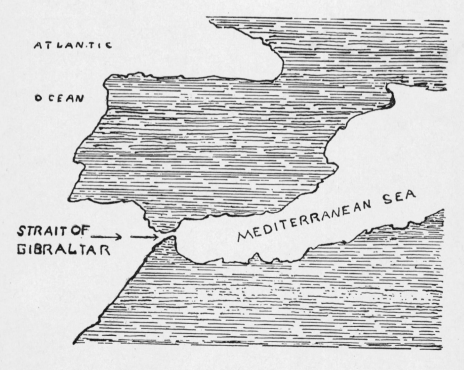

During the last war, German submarines took advantage of these unusual currents to get past the great fortress of Gibraltar, where the British were on guard. The enemy submarines would submerge a short distance below the water's surface, cut off their engines and float into the Mediterranean with the incoming current. Then, on their way back into the Atlantic, the submarines would submerge deeper and be carried by the outgoing Mediterranean current, silently and unseen, below the British warships. So you see, a knowledge of the ocean and its currents can be useful in many different ways.

There are two currents in the Strait of Gibraltar, each going in an opposite direction.

Good and Bad Winds

When you go to the beach during the hot days of summer, you will probably find hundreds of others there, too, all trying to cool off in the breeze blowing from the ocean. How lucky you are if you can spend all summer by the seashore! And you will probably enjoy the cool ocean breezes even more if you understand a little of how they come about.

When the sun beats down on the earth, it heats the air quickly, often making places in some parts of the world's deserts too hot for humans to live in them. But when the sun beats down on the ocean, the water absorbs, or takes in the heat. A very long time is required to warm this water. Scientists tell us that water needs three thousand times more heat to warm it than is required to heat air. Not only can the ocean absorb a great amount of *heat* from the air and hold it but it can also absorb and hold a greater amount of *cold* and hold it than does the air. So it is not surprising that, even on the hottest day ashore, the ocean is able to send out cool breezes from its vast storehouse of colder-than-air waters. This is nature's own air conditioning and heating system, and it has provided cool or warm air in this way for thousands of years.

Ocean currents, too, help control the breezes from the ocean. Not only do these currents, moving from the equatorial regions, carry heat from the tropics to cold areas, but the cold currents coming from the polar regions carry with them cold waters which help to cool the hot temperatures of certain land areas.

The sea, covering three-fourths of our earth as it does, is the regulator of our climate, causing good and bad, hot or cold, wet or dry weather. The sea makes you think of a fairybook genie that performs marvels. But, of course, there are many questions that still remain unanswered concerning, not only the effect of oceans on the climate of the world but also the reasons for currents, tides and many other remarkable and strange wonders of the deep sea.

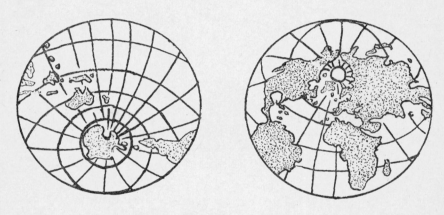

The sea covers three-quarters of our earth.

Over the miles of ocean there are many types of winds. Some bring disaster, others are kind. You have already read about how calm it usually is in some places, such as over the Sargasso Sea. In locations like the South Polar region, there are tremendous winds, so dreaded that, in the days of sailing ships, they were given the name of "roaring forties," meaning that the wind blew with terrific force near latitude forty. In olden days, sailing vessels depended entirely upon favorable winds in order to get to where there was trade. That is why the helpful winds that blow quite regularly from both sides of the equator, where the earth spin is greatest, were

45

given the name of "trade winds." Between the trade winds of the Northern and Southern Hemispheres, there is a belt of calm, with hot, sultry air known as the "doldrums." Around the outer edge of the trade winds are found light winds but, unlike the doldrums, here the periods of calm do not last for long. Strangely enough, this location is called the "horse latitudes" because, some say, sailing vessels carrying horses from Europe to the New World were becalmed in this area. When the feed for these animals ran out, the sailors threw them into the sea.

In Africa and Asia, seasonal winds known as "monsoons" arise from the terrific difference in temperature between land and ocean. Very often they blow fiercely and approach the force of a gale. In certain areas of the world, there are local winds which blow strongly upon the ocean. For example, in Hawaii there are "Kona" winds which come sweeping from the south; in the southern part of South America a "Williwaw" is a violent burst of wind suddenly swooping down from the mountains; in California, a "Santa Ana" wind comes roaring from the coast out over the sea.

The most feared winds of the oceans are those that occur during cyclones. In the Pacific Ocean they are called typhoons and in the Atlantic they are known as hurricanes. Both are the same type of wind but a typhoon can stretch over three to four times the area that a hurricane usually spans.

Anyone who lives on the Eastern or the Gulf Coast of the United States knows how serious hurricanes can be. From the time one is first born as a small, suspicious area until it blows into monstrous, raging winds, radio and TV programs and newspapers warn everybody in the path of a hurricane.

These cyclonic winds usually begin somewhere in the southern part of the Gulf of Mexico or in the southern half of the North Atlantic Ocean. Air flowing toward a center of low pressure is shifted off its course by the earth's rotation and, as a result, it moves in a spiral path toward the low pressure point. Round it goes, faster and faster, as the whole wind mass moves slowly across the sea, quite often headed toward land. Since such winds can move within the circle of their path as fast as one hundred and fifty miles an hour, or more, there is great danger to people and property in the way of these gigantic storms.

The waves stirred up by a hurricane often become as high as a tall building but, right in the center of this whirling mass of air, is a calm spot called the "eye," where there are no waves or wind at all. When a hurricane strikes you, you might feel its full force for hours as the wind mass advances slowly. Then, if you are in the center of its path, the eye will pass over you and you might think you are safe, for there will be a dead calm. But very soon, more winds from the rear half of the hurricane will begin to blast and you must take shelter from it once again.

Fearless pilots of the United States Armed Forces fly into the eye of a hurricane in order to chart its course and send warnings on ahead as to the path it will take. Many lives have been saved because of this hurricane hunting service.

Besides the terrible winds of a hurricane, there sometimes occurs on the ocean another destructive wind — a waterspout. You probably have heard of tornadoes ripping across land. Well, a waterspout is about the same type of wind but it takes place on the sea. It never becomes quite so large or destructive as a tornado but it

Some waves are as high as a tall building.

picks up water in its whirling five-hundred-miles-an-hour winds, spouting it high in the air.

On calm days, in warm seas, it is not unusual to see several water-spouts at one time. If you are in a boat, it is wise to do what you can to keep out of their way. Sailing ship captains fear waterspouts because, with their slow-moving vessels, they have no means of getting away from them in time. You will never guess what these captains sometimes do when waterspouts come near their ships. They try to break them up when they approach by shooting at them with shotguns. And it is said this often works!

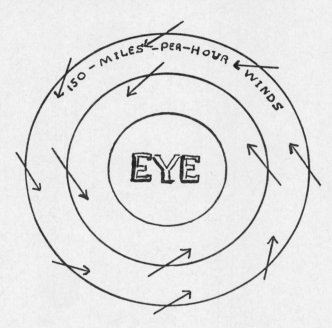

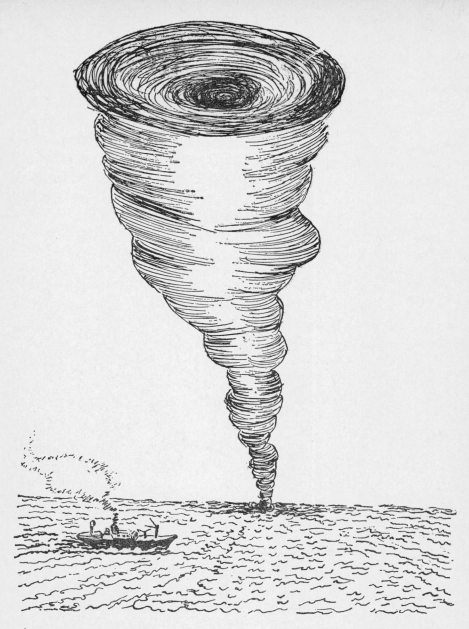

A waterspout sometimes whirls at the dangerous speed of five hundred miles an hour.

Waves

There are many kinds of waves in the ocean. Some pound rocky coasts, grinding rock against rock, gradually wearing away cliffs like a giant bulldozer. Still other waves are feared by all men for they are powerful enough to not only toss mighty ocean liners about with ease, but often bring death and destruction to people and property along coast lines. Waves can also be beneficial in many ways, such as moving the sand in the ocean to build sand bars and adding land to shore lines. There are all sorts of waves but it might be interesting to know first how waves are formed.

It is easy to make waves yourself. Just jump into a swimming pool and watch the water speed across to the sides in rolling waves. In the ocean, however, there is seldom anything falling that would be large enough to cause a noticeable wave in such a vast area. Rather, waves are, for the most part, caused by wind which blows at the ocean water until, instead of it having a flat surface, as water normally does, it is pushed into a series of "troughs," which are the hollows between waves, and "crests," which are the tops of waves. In the deep ocean, the wave form passes through the surface water, moving it up and down. The water does not move forward normally. You can prove this by placing a cork in a swimming pool where there are waves. The cork bounces up and down with the waves but does not come any closer to you. However, when a violent storm rages at sea and the winds are so fierce that they have the force to push the water ahead of them, creating towering waves, then the wave form will move forward, in addition to the way it usually moves, up and down.

When these waves move toward shallow water or shore lines, they are slowed down by the solid earth or rocks beneath, which drags at them like a brake. This causes the waves, or "breakers" as they are called now, to slow down beneath the water while on the surface, the wind still pushes them, crowding them forward, piling them up behind one another. Very often you can hardly stand up in front of these waves as they thunder shoreward. Finally, the breakers topple, curl and crash, rushing ahead as if in a terrible hurry to get somewhere. At this point they are called "surf."

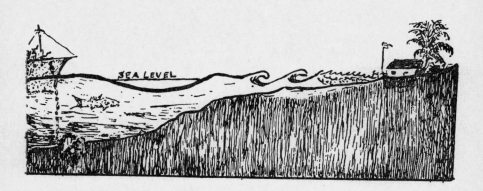

As waves move toward shore lines, they are slowed down by the solid earth beneath them.

Another reason for waves toppling in foaming white-caps is because, in the open sea, driven by wind, these storm waves pile so high on the surface of the deep water that finally they become top heavy and fall down, just as anything else would that you might pile too high.

51

Waves from nearby storms can pound sandy beaches unmercifully and cause tremendous damage. To give you an idea of the strength of waves as they move over shallow water — a solid block of concrete weighing four thousand five hundred pounds was moved twelve feet and turned over on its side by waves no more than four feet high.

During a severe storm in France, over one hundred years ago, in a port city, stones from a breakwater weighing nearly seven thousand pounds were thrown over a wall twenty feet high. In England, a great block of cement, resting on stones and bound by iron rods, all of which together weighed one thousand three hundred and fifty tons, was torn from its place by waves and dropped in another spot. The people in this English seacoast town put their heads together and decided that the next time a storm came they would have something ready so that no waves on earth could destroy it. So they substituted for the old block of cement one weighing two thousand six hundred tons — more than five million pounds — and this, too, was later carried away by storm waves!

A block of cement weighing five million pounds was carried away by storm waves.

It may take many years but, by constant pounding, waves sometimes wash away mountains and change shore lines. Or they may even build up islands. In Holland, dikes are built to keep the sea from taking any more of the low-lying land and covering it with water. Even cliffs may tumble down from the persistent beating of waves and whole towns, perched high above the water, have been known to become undermined and fall into the sea.

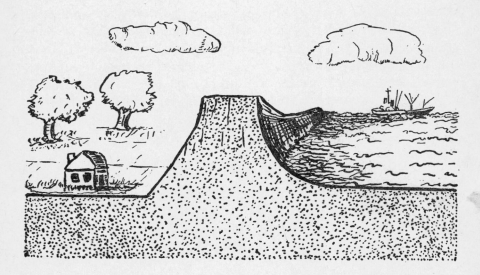

In Holland, dikes are built to hold back the sea.

The most dangerous of all waves are those caused by under-water earthquakes and volcanoes. You have already read about the disaster a wall of water eighty feet high once caused to countries in the South Pacific Ocean. But did you know that waves from underwater earthquakes can travel across the open sea at fantastic rates of speed? There is a record of a wave which traveled nine hundred miles an hour! Naturally, when these mighty waves strike the coast, great damage follows. In 1868, a United States warship was carried a quarter of a mile over the land by a large wave caused by an earthquake many miles away. You can imagine how the sailors felt at being transported on their ship over land — and then, when the wave went out, to find themselves high and dry! The warship remained in the same spot until still another wave carried it even farther inland. This gives you a pretty good idea as to the power of waves.

A large wave carried a warship a quarter of a mile inland.

IV
THE OCEAN
AND ITS MYSTERIES

Exploring the Ocean Depths

Usually the question everyone asks when seeing the ocean for the first time is: "How deep is it?"

When we look at the surface, there is no clue to the question of "how deep" — which is a very important one in many ways. Boats of various sizes require enough water beneath them before they can move safely. Fishermen must know how deep the water is to best locate the schools of fish. And scientists want to find out about the water depth so that they can map out the undersea continents, as they have already done with the continents above water.

The deepest place yet found in all the oceans of the world is called the Marianas Trench. This is far away in the Pacific Ocean, near the island of Guam. Here, the water is thirty-five thousand, nine hundred and forty-eight feet deep — over six and a half miles straight down! When you realize that most of us are over our heads when standing in water just six feet deep, you can understand why it is so hard for you to imagine all that water.

The deep spots in the ocean floor are not reached suddenly. Continents are surrounded by bands of shallow water areas called "continental shelves." These shelves slope gently and gradually from shore lines. If you will turn a dinner plate upside down, its sloping edges will look very much like a continental shelf. The depth of the water over these shelving areas is usually more than four hundred feet. In the Antarctic regions, the water is two thousand feet deep above this shelf, but still not as deep as the sea beyond it.

The outermost edge of a shelf plunges down steeply, and this is called the "continental slope." These continental slopes are found at a distance of thirty to many hundreds of miles from shore lines. Some slopes have a sheer drop downward of two miles. One slope has a drop of five miles and if you stood on the edge of this high cliff, looking down, it would be difficult to see bottom.

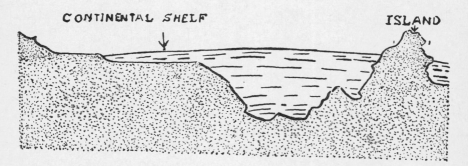

Depths greater than one thousand fathoms — a fathom being six feet — are called "abyssal" regions. Then if you descend still farther, you are in the "deeps," which occur below three thousand fathoms. There are also great gouges or slashes in the ocean floor that are over four thousand fathoms deep. The scientists call these deepest places "trenches." They make the largest canyons in the world look tiny by comparison.

Now that you have found out how really deep the ocean is, the next questions you will probably ask are, "What is hidden by all the miles and miles of water? What is it like down in the ocean depths?"

You would never guess at some of the amazing, wonderful secrets underneath the thousands of miles of open ocean! There are high mountains, wide valleys, deep canyons and dark caves and vast barren deserts of sand. Enormous fishes roam the oceans like gypsies, sometimes swimming through miles of floating plankton. Nearer to shore are jungles of seaweed with all kinds of queer-looking creatures lurking in the shadows and tiny, brightly-colored fishes, hiding in rock coral. Some of the undersea places are a fairyland of fantastic beauty, while the unexplored depths hold the mystery of a strange, unknown world.

For hundreds of years, men have been trying to see what lies beneath the surface of the ocean. Many fearless divers have investigated some of the shallower marine areas using tons of expensive equipment, in attempts to solve some of the oceans' secrets.

Probably the first man to study the undersea world scientifically was Alexander the Great. Not much is known of his submarine adventures but he is supposed to have gone beneath the water's surface in a crude apparatus that enabled him to look around a little. He was only able to report on seeing a few fishes.

Leonardo da Vinci was concerned with ocean diving and he sketched many kinds of equipment which, unfortunately, were never built. Then in 1825, a man stayed below the surface of the water successfully. In 1872, still another attempt was made, but in both cases the apparatus was not the right kind to make undersea diving practical.

Many people tried to perfect underwater equipment that would enable them to stay below the surface long enough to examine the undersea world thoroughly, but for a great many years, no one could discover just how this might be done. The people who knew the most about the ocean floor were pearl divers and sponge fishermen who made their living by diving, fairly deep, below the surface of the sea. However, they depended upon the air they were able to hold in their lungs for breathing, and this naturally limited their stay underneath, so the real secrets of the submarine world lay un-discovered for a great number of years.

Diving suits finally came into existence, but these earliest clumsy, heavy contraptions required a boat equipped with a crew working an air pump and they were too hazardous for people to use without being well trained.

It was not until 1943 that two Frenchmen, Cousteau and Gagnan, solved the problem that had been puzzling men for hundreds of years — how to enable a man to stay below the water's surface with no help from above. They pumped air into metal bottles which were attached to a diver's back. Two tubes connected the bottles to the diver's mouth and there was a valve in between to regulate the flow of air. This gadget was named an aqua-lung.

A diver wearing an aqua-lung.

At last! All a man had to do was strap this equipment to him, follow simple instructions and dive below the surface, where he could swim around, almost like a fish, until the bottled air was used up. Of course, he was limited as to the depth he could descend because of the tremendous pressure down below. An aqua-lung diver can descend below the surface as deep down as 300 feet.

In addition to the aqua-lung, a diver is equipped with a glass face mask, enclosing his eyes and nose, and a pair of rubber fins that slip over his feet and look very much like the webbed feet of a frog. The fins help him to move faster in the water.

The inexpensive aqua lung was sold to people of many countries. Soon the undersea world began to give up some of the secrets it had guarded for thousands of years. Divers exploring found the ocean floor more marvelous than anyone had imagined. There are reefs made of giant fields of towering coral, growing in all possible shapes, sizes and colors — some formations looking like mushrooms, trees or beautiful flowers. There are also unusual seaweeds and brightly colored fishes darting about. In many of the world's warm waters some of these wonders may be found close to shore.

KELP

SARGASSUM

IRISH MOSS

Off the eastern coast of Australia is located a diver's paradise. It is a tremendous coral reef, known as the Great Barrier Reef, and it is over one thousand miles long. This reef lies anywhere from twenty to one hundred miles out from shore, but there are other closer-in reefs, such as those which can be found as near as ten feet from the Florida shore. You can imagine how many billions of tiny animals it took to build all this coral!

Even though today heavy diving suits are not used by as many people as those using the aqua-lung, they are indispensable in many kinds of undersea work and scientific explorations. There are deep-sea divers who regularly carry on underwater salvage and repair work on such things as ships and docks, while in some countries sponges are gathered from the ocean bottom as deep down as five hundred and forty feet, by men wearing these diving suits. This kind of professional deep-sea diving requires great skill and experience. Many fine discoveries can be credited to the use of these diving suits.

It is not easy to explore the deeper places of the ocean, for the pressure on an object a mile below is around a ton for every square inch of surface. Still deeper down, the pressure increases. Some day, a way will probably be discovered which will enable humans to withstand the tremendous pressures of the black, cold, six-and-a-half-mile depths. Steps have been taken in that direction already, for in 1934, a thick metal container called a bathysphere was lowered into the sea by cable from a ship off Bermuda. Dr. William Beebe and an assistant were sealed inside it and they descended three thousand twenty-eight feet — over one-half mile.

When they were one hundred and fifty feet below the surface in the bathysphere, they found that the sunlight had faded and the water had taken on a blue, misty light. At four hundred feet, this light had dwindled and it was too dark to read. When they were nineteen hundred feet down, it became pitch black and extremely cold. Powerful lights shining through the heavy glass windows in the bathysphere pierced the blackness at this depth.

This kind of ocean exploring is found to be much more satisfactory than using diving suits, for the men in the bathysphere can

61

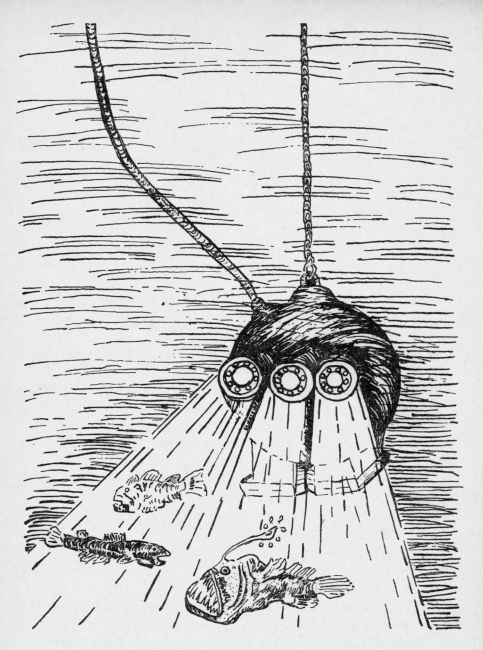

This bathysphere took Dr. Beebe over one-half mile below the surface.

stay in the depths long enough to take notes and make drawings of what they see, without suffering any ill effects. And especially, they are able to descend much deeper than anyone can in a diving suit.

Among many scientific findings, Dr. Beebe discovered strange fishes that had never been seen before. He found that this dark world, between the ocean's bottom and its surface, has no plants and that the creatures down there are able to produce their own light — called phosphorescence. This lights up various parts of their bodies. It is similar to the way fireflies glow. These fishes always stay in their own level of the ocean, for they cannot stand the difference in pressure either below or above it.

The benthoscope was the next invention used to explore the ocean depths. In 1949, Otis Barton, in a round metal container, descended four thousand five hundred feet — nearly a mile below the surface — off the California coast.

The Swiss scientist Auguste Piccard and his son went down almost two miles below the surface of the Mediterranean Sea in their bathyscaphe in 1953.

Then in 1954, two Frenchmen, Lieutenant Commander Georges Houot and Lieutenant Pierre-Henri Wilm, set the record of all time when they descended into the ocean off the African coast thirteen thousand, two hundred and eighty-seven feet — over two and a half miles! They used a very wonderful deep sea machine called a bathyscaphe. These two scientists expect to descend even farther some day.

It would be a true adventure to go along on one of these trips — to explore below the water's surface and see the odd creatures living down so deep. It is an exciting way to learn new things about the wonders of the wonderful ocean.

Another remarkable way of descending below the surface is in a submarine. These metal undersea craft are used by governments for defense and exploration.

In 1958, the atomic powered submarine *Nautilus* cruised beneath the almost solid packs of ice of the Arctic ice cap, staying below the surface five and a half days, for a depth of more than four hundred feet.

63

Another submarine, the *Sea Wolf*, logged fifteen thousand seven hundred nautical miles, staying below the water's surface for sixty days. Both of these feats are something that have never been done before.

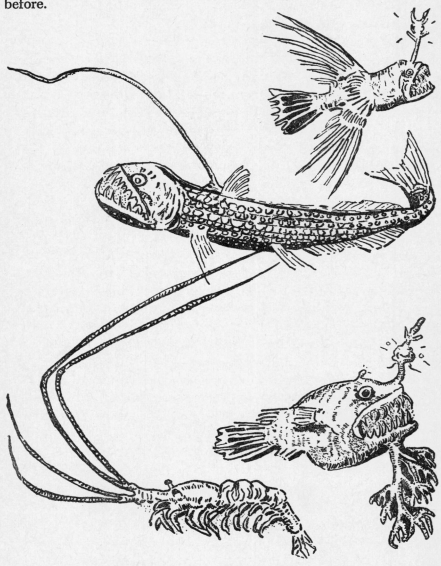

There are many strange fish in the deep sea.

Being on these submarines, while they prowled the ocean, not to be able to see the sun or the blue sky for the many days they remained below, must have been both exciting and frightening. But these voyages of exploration will do a great deal to help unravel some of the mysteries in the deep sea.

Knowledge of the very deep-down sea floor — two and a half miles deeper — comes to us from scientists who have discovered many important things. This has been achieved mainly by using sensitive flash cameras lowered to the sea bottom, from collecting samples of matter there and by using instruments such as fathometers, which tell you the depth and contour of the ocean floor. By these methods, a sort of map of the undersea world is being made.

Although the bottom of the ocean is almost freezing cold and in total darkness, certain things are seen by dredging and bringing bottom samples to the surface. It has been found that queer kinds of crabs called sea spiders, sea worms, odd squid and fish dwell there.

All of the undersea world is not interesting. Besides the mountains and valleys, there are desolate expanses of sand, just like our deserts on land. And the rocklike lava of the volcanic cones which are so very numerous in the Pacific Ocean, forms an important part of the sea bottom. Most of these cones are so far beneath the surface that, if they erupted and spewed out volcanic rocks, a ship sailing above them might not even know about it.

If you were hiking across the ocean floor, you would not find it much fun when you came to the "bottom ooze" or "clay" and sank down into the sticky stuff. The oozes and clays were formed by billions of tiny and large dead creatures of the sea, along with shells, seaweed and everything else that might sink to the bottom, all piling up on one another for millions of years, ever since the oceans began to teem with life. Some of the oozes and clays are thousands of feet deep. It may surprise you to hear that you can easily squeeze the ooze through your fingers while it is wet but, when exposed to air, it will become as hard as rock.

Lost Continents

There are some things the deep sea might be hiding that would startle everyone if they were suddenly found — and if they were found, many of our ideas and legends about old civilizations might quickly change to fact. One of these legends that has been handed down to us through the centuries is about the large, lost continent of Atlantis. This is supposed to have existed in the Atlantic Ocean, outside the Straits of Gibraltar. Quite intelligent farmers and sea-farers were believed to have lived on this continent.

Of course, you are wondering what is thought to have happened to Atlantis and why it is no longer part of our world. Well, if you will remember our earth's crust wrinkling up like a dried prune, you will, perhaps, have a clue as to the disappearing Atlantis. Changes in the earth's crust might have caused this ocean continent suddenly to sink from sight. As an indication that this could have happened, some point to the 1950 earthquake in India that was strong enough to change the course of rivers, drain and create lakes, ruin settled communities and raise the height of the Himalaya Mountains close to two hundred feet.

Scientists also point to the gradually sinking continent of Greenland and to Sweden, Finland and parts of Russia which have risen several feet in the last century. Also, the Straits of Gibraltar have spread in the last two thousand years from about one mile to fifteen miles wide. So if these changes to the earth's surface are actually happening in our time, it is not difficult to believe that, in an earlier age, when the face of the earth was wrinkling very often, whole continents could sink beneath the sea.

There are other unexplained things about the crust of the earth and its oceans. One of these is a gigantic mountain chain extending across the bottom of the Atlantic Ocean. Called the "mid-Atlantic ridge," this mountain range is about ten thousand miles long, reaching from an area near Iceland in the north to a spot near Antarctica in the south. Most of these mountains lie buried a mile below the sea, but a few of the highest peaks are sticking up above the water. Some of these are the island of Pico in the Azores, St. Paul's Rocks between Brazil and Africa and many islands in the Polar region. It is interesting to imagine that this enormous undersea chain of mountains could once have been above the water like the Rocky Mountains and Andes are now.

Whatever may be the answer to these riddles that have puzzled scientists for many years, we hope that, with the discovery of various advanced methods and equipment to add to the ones we already have, men will be able to descend to the deepest part of the ocean and learn the truth about Atlantis and any other continents that could have been covered with water many thousands of years ago.

Voyages

From the time that primitive man stood on the shore, looking toward the ocean, until nowadays, when we go to the beach and gaze out over the waves, many puzzling questions about the great sea have arisen. For example, no one can spot a small floating object over three miles away. This same is also true on a prairie. The reason for this is that, from where we stand on the ground, the curve of the earth's surface prevents us from seeing very far. But if we climb a mountain or go up in a plane to a ten-thousand-foot height we can see as far as one hundred and thirty-two miles away. This, of course, is a very short distance to see on an ocean when there are so many thousands of miles of it.

Our ancestors had such terrific problems of survival that they never explored the ocean waters. Most of their time was spent in hunting for food, staying warm and protecting themselves from

Primitive men had to protect themselves from the fierce animals that roamed the earth.

attack by the fierce animals that roamed the earth. This is probably the reason why early man had no knowledge of ocean boats and ocean travel. The sea was much more of a mystery then than it is now.

Later, there were men in the world who were not satisfied with just eating, sleeping and fighting. They wanted to learn what was in the ocean beyond the little that they could see from the shore. Probably fishermen, blown away from the safe coastal waters, returned to tell tales of odd fish, tremendous waves and vicious winds — and these tales fired the curiosity of their families and neighbors about the sea until, finally, the first ocean voyages came about.

As you probably already know, long trips at sea and the discovery of new continents did not start with Columbus and Magellan, for they were not the first ones to explore the lonely oceans. People were sailing vast distances twenty-five hundred years before Columbus was born!

These early seafarers were called Phoenicians and, from 1000 B.C. to 100 B.C., they lived on the eastern coast of the Mediterranean Sea. We do not know exactly when ocean travel started among these people but we do know they were great traders. Voyages often took them west across the Mediterranean, out through the Gates of Hercules (now called the Straits of Gibraltar) and into the Atlantic Ocean. These hardy seafarers explored the coasts of Europe and Africa and established many cities along their shores. Other Phoenician boats are supposed to have traveled south through the Red Sea, into the Indian Ocean and all around the southern tip of Africa into the Atlantic Ocean. Then, sailing up the west coast of Africa, they eventually found their way home by going back into the Mediterranean, through the Straits of Gibraltar.

If you had been along on any of those perilous journeys across uncharted waters, you would most likely have been just as frightened as the early explorers were. The thousands of miles of ocean held unknown dangers and, besides, the earth was believed to be flat, just like the top of a table. Most everyone was afraid to venture any farther than his own shore lines. People thought that, if they

Early voyagers believed the world was flat and that their ship would fall off at the horizon.

sailed out to the horizon — which is where water and sky seem to meet — their flat world ended and they would surely tumble off into space. It took great courage for those first adventurers to learn about the ocean firsthand.

Six hundred years after the birth of Christ, Irish monks traveled from their homes by boat across the Atlantic to such places as Iceland and even Greenland. When those warrior-sailors, the Vikings, later sailed to Iceland, they found that the Irish had landed there first.

The Vikings came from the coast of Norway. They went to sea to find new land and to seek trade. They crossed the Norwegian Sea in their open sailing vessels and established settlements in Iceland and Greenland. In the year 1000, the Vikings discovered the continent that was later to be known as the United States.

Remember, in those days there were no canned goods to take on long journeys and enough fresh water, bulky food and fighting weapons had to be carried on the small vessels to keep 'the men aboard healthy and well-armed for their conquests in strange lands. Perhaps you are thinking, "What fun to have been on those early voyages of exploration and discovery!" But going on these journeys also meant hardship, privation and suffering. Do not think it was an easy life or all fun.

During the thirteenth, fourteenth and fifteenth centuries, England, Italy, Spain and Portugal began getting interested in the rest of the unknown world and they sent out ships to investigate. But not until the year 1415 was there a man who really gave impetus to the exploration of faraway places. Prince Henry the Navigator, born in Portugal, became known as probably the greatest of all discoverers, even though he never commanded a ship himself.

Prince Henry mastered the arts of mathematics and navigation and saw to it that Portugal, his country, built the best ships afloat. He was not the kind of man to depend on chance. He figured everything out perfectly so that nothing within his power could go wrong. Eventually, his sea captains brought in more and more information on navigation, until, finally, two of his men finished long, remarkable voyages. Bartolomeo Diaz rounded the southern tip of Africa

A Viking ship

and Vasco da Gama, following the tracks of Diaz, made his historic trip to India.

Later, other captains discovered the now famous Newfoundland codfishing banks — which are shallow places in the surrounding deep ocean.

All of Prince Henry's calculations on navigation helped lead up to the greatest find of all — the discovery of North America later, in 1492, by another excellent navigator, Christopher Columbus. Prince Henry's captains had crossed the Atlantic Ocean, using the Gulf Stream current as they traveled the seaways. They made it possible for later explorers to find a whole new continent that people eventually developed into a great country.

In 1519, another great navigator, Ferdinand Magellan, led the first expedition around the world. He left Sanlucar, Spain, sailed down the coast of South America, then through a passage in the islands at the tip of South America — now called the Strait of Magellan — then headed northwest across the Pacific, touching the Marianas Islands. He then went west of the Philippines but was killed there; his men sailed down through the Indonesian Islands, across the Indian Ocean and finally up the west coast of Africa and back to Spain. At last it was proved that man could travel completely around the world without falling off into space.

You are probably wondering what was happening on the largest and deepest ocean of all, the Pacific, during all this time when the Atlantic and Indian Oceans were being explored. Was this vast body of water being ignored or were curious people exploring it, too?

The answer to these questions is that, before Magellan was ever to see the Pacific, natives of the Polynesian Islands were traveling on this ocean as though it were a wide, long road. We are not sure when such voyages started, but we do know that these natives must have been excellent sailors to travel from one island to another without the aid of any of the guiding instruments used later by European navigators. Moreover, the South Sea islanders made these long trips in small, open boats.

As far as we know, these great seamen of the Pacific depended entirely on migrating birds and on the stars for a knowledge of where they were heading on the uncharted ocean. As they gradually learned more about the stars, these adventurers were able to sail farther and farther beyond their own islands, covering thousands of miles of ocean. They used double dugout canoes called catamarans, in which they carried their families, coconuts, pigs, cooking utensils, fresh water and many other things that would be useful in settling on a new island. They were intelligent, brave people who loved the sea and completely depended upon it for their transportation.

Natives of the Polynesian Islands were the first voyagers on the Pacific Ocean.

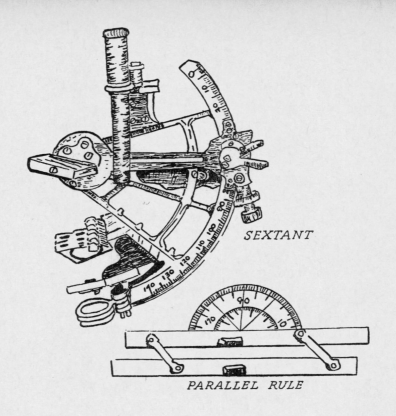

SEXTANT

PARALLEL RULE

Dangers and Adventures

As men became braver and covered more space on the oceans, their findings were carefully put down in the ship's log — the day by day account of everything that happened at sea, including the exact location, at all times, of the vessel they were sailing. The important information contained in these logs was later put into books which we study now. This is one of the chief reasons why the sea captains of today do not have to travel across the oceans as they used to, following a series of guesses.

Also, great inventions and aids to navigation have been made available since the first explorers set out on their hazardous voyages, so now boats rarely get lost.

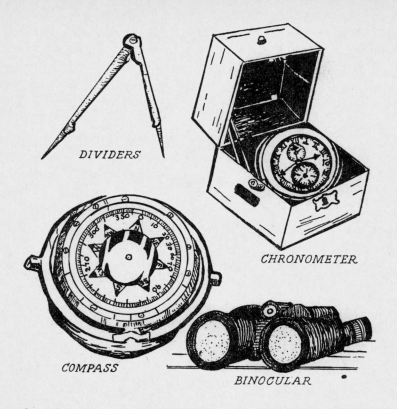

DIVIDERS

CHRONOMETER

COMPASS

BINOCULAR

Besides the necessary compass, chronometer, sextant, parallel rules and dividers, there are also other aids to navigation. A chart — which is like a land map, only it deals with the ocean — is very important, for it tells the navigator where he will find shallow and deep water, rocks and reefs. Current and tide tables are also necessary in navigating a ship and binoculars help those in charge to see things more clearly in the distance, by night or by day. Radar can pick out and locate objects ahead of a ship and in this way help to avoid collisions. Loran, a remarkable system of navigation using a radio wave, tells the captain where he is at any time. The short-wave radio enables those on board a ship to talk with people in other parts of the world and to get help or storm information whenever needed. Fathometers tell captains how much water is beneath them at all times, so there is less danger of running aground.

Although we have wonderful navigational instruments and the warnings of buoys, foghorns and lighthouses to help us keep safe at sea, just the same, every good captain is always on the alert. Unexpected happenings on the ocean are still plentiful enough to make ships proceed with caution.

One of the real terrors of the ocean is the iceberg. Many ships, not equipped with radar, have been wrecked by these huge mountains of ice that break off from glaciers and drift down from the Arctic region. The Labrador Current carries these icebergs into the shipping lanes of the North Atlantic, where they often last for a year or more, until the warm waters of the Gulf Stream finally melt them.

Some icebergs have been found to be enormous — twenty miles wide and seventy miles long, with a depth of twenty-five hundred feet — two hundred and seventy feet of this rising above the water and the rest, one thousand two hundred and thirty feet, being below the surface. If you could ride horseback across an iceberg that big, it would take you a whole day, figuring that the average horse walks at the rate of about ten miles an hour, for the animal would probably be unable to gallop over the slippery surface.

Many people have been fooled by icebergs, for often they look like islands. These great masses of ice are so brittle that the shot of a gun will often split them. Sailors know this and keep their distance, for a crashing iceberg that has been split in two can send out waves that could swamp even a large vessel easily.

There have been great disasters caused by icebergs. One night in 1912, the *Titanic*, at that time the world's largest ship, was in the North Atlantic. It was a foggy night. Suddenly, a great white shape loomed up in front of the vessel. With a terrible shuddering and crunching, the *Titanic* struck an iceberg, ripping open her hull. Before help could come from nearby ships, the *Titanic* went to the bottom, carrying one thousand five hundred and seventeen people with her.

As a result of this disaster, ice patrols are maintained by some governments. These scouting patrols chart the large icebergs and

Some icebergs are enormous.

radio their positions to all ships at sea, so that the captains can steer clear of them.

In spite of icebergs, dangerous storm waves, gale winds and treacherous currents, the oceans are no longer nearly as frightening to sailors as they were many years ago. At any time nowadays, hundreds of ships are using the sea lanes. Even quite small boats will often undertake an ocean passage.

Round the world travel in small boats was proved possible when, in 1895, Captain Joshua Slocum left Boston, Massachusetts, all alone in his thirty-seven-foot sailboat, *The Spray*. He completed a forty-six-thousand-mile sea voyage by way of Nova Scotia, Gibraltar, South America, the Straits of Magellan, the South Seas and Africa, arriving at Newport, Rhode Island, in 1898. He reached home, perfectly safe and sound, three years after he had started, and one year of this time was spent in stopovers at various ports.

Since then, others have crossed oceans and gone around the world in boats of all sizes and types. One man even crossed the

A rubber raft has been used to cross the Atlantic Ocean.

Atlantic Ocean all alone in a rubber boat that measured hardly longer than himself. Maybe one day somebody will even try to cross the ocean in a washtub! Do you remember the old nursery rhyme about the three men who went to sea in a tub?

Of course, there are dangers to voyaging on the open sea, if you are foolhardy and careless. Some very excellent boats have been lost and never heard from again and there are also mysteries concerning ships on the sea so baffling that now, many years after they happened, people are still wondering about them.

"Rub - a - dub - dub,
Three men in a tub!"

One of the strangest of all these is the puzzle of the Brigantine *Mary Celeste*. More stories have been written about this ship than about any other craft that ever sailed the seas!

The mystery of the *Mary Celeste* starts over eighty-five years ago, when she was found off the Azores without any crew aboard. The most surprising thing about the affair is that the brigantine was traveling along with part of her sails up, yet not one single person could be found on or near her. There were no lifeboats aboard. Rusty swords and signs of fighting were found, which indicated there must have been a tragedy of some sort. Many people think that the crew killed all the officers and then got away in a lifeboat, all of them dying at sea. Others think that something frightened everyone on board and they all hurried to get off the ship, leaving the sails up in their haste. Then, when they thought it was safe to return, a wind came up and the *Mary Celeste* sailed off without them. No one knows the true answer for neither the captain, his wife and small daughter nor any of the crew were ever heard from again. What do *you* think happened to the *Mary Celeste?*

An odd voyage took place in 1947, on a forty-five-foot raft made of balsa wood. Six men left the South American port of Callao, Peru, on this raft and, pushed by winds and currents from the east, they were carried westward across the Pacific Ocean. Finally, after one hundred and one days, they landed at Raroia, Polynesia, one of the many small islands scattered over the ocean in this part of the world. The name of this raft was the *Kon-Tiki* and the men aboard demonstrated that it was possible to travel hundreds of miles, pushed by ocean currents and wind, in probably the same way that early seafarers did, when they might have settled the various islands of the South Pacific.

Many people thought the frail raft would never make the trip safely, for even large ships with powerful engines have difficulty at times from strong winds and high waves. It is remarkable, but this raft did finish its four-thousand-three-hundred-mile trip successfully after one of the most daring ocean voyages known to history.

Kon - Tiki

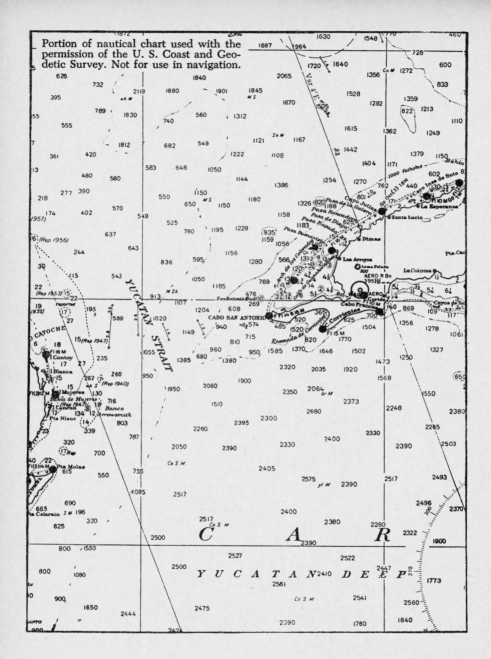

Portion of nautical chart used with the permission of the U. S. Coast and Geodetic Survey. Not for use in navigation.

A chart is an important aid to navigation.

V
YOU AND
THE OCEAN

Undersea Treasure

Would you believe that billions of dollars worth of gold, silver and precious gems are at the bottom of the sea? Treasure hunters all over the world know this and are constantly examining maps and charts, trying to pin point locations, before starting out on expeditions to find some of this wealth. And it might surprise you to know that most of the world's sunken treasure is in waters near the United States.

When Spain was colonizing the New World, the Indians of the Americas had to pay tribute to their masters in the form of valuables. Spanish boats would travel from port to port in the Caribbean Sea, making collections of the gold and silver that were mined in these countries. After filling their ships to capacity, the Spanish captains headed out to sea with millions of dollars' worth of bounty in each vessel.

Unfortunately, in those early days of navigation, little was known about all the reefs in this part of the world. Often, if sudden hurricanes blew up, these vessels would be swept upon the jagged coral. In a short time, the waves pounded the ships to pieces and they sank. The crew considered themselves lucky if they escaped with their lives. The treasure, bound for the New World, was nearly always left behind in large chests, where most of it still rests, immersed in sea water.

Also, you will remember that there were pirates in these waters. Men like Captain Kidd, Bluebeard and Henry Morgan repeatedly attacked and sank these treasure-laden Spanish galleons. Sometimes these thieves were able to carry off the Spanish gold and silver. More often than not, the pirates fought over the treasure themselves, boats were scuttled and many times the treasure found its way to the bottom of the sea.

Since the year 1500, nearly one million vessels have been lost at sea from one cause or another. We know the exact spot where some went down, but there are many more that sank without leaving a trace of their whereabouts. Not all of these ships were carrying Spanish treasure when they went to the bottom. Some had coins of gold and silver to pay the crew at various points on the trip. All together, so much gold and silver has been lost at sea it is said that one quarter of all that has been mined in the world is now resting somewhere in a watery grave.

Many treasure seekers have searched for — and sometimes found — this undersea wealth. These hunters of the deep often have sensitive instruments that tell them if there is metal underneath the boat from which they hunt. Whenever metal is indicated, over the side they go, in diving suits or with aqua-lungs strapped to their backs.

If a diver goes down for treasure and the water is clear, he may see the awesome skeleton of a Spanish galleon, with its cannons, anchors and other fittings completely covered with coral. Often it is necessary to pry and hack away hundreds of years of coral growth before the treasure chest is finally found.

Sunken gold is certainly not a myth, for there have been many important finds such as a treasure chest off Cuba containing sixty thousand dollars in coin; gold and silver bars worth forty thousand dollars from a wreck off Peru; a Dutch frigate that yielded sixty-nine thousand dollars' worth of treasure; and a Spanish galleon sunk in the Bahamas whose silver and gold bars were worth twenty thousand dollars.

All this sunken treasure was retrieved by deep-sea hunters, just as you might if, some day, you went looking for valuables in the ocean.

Bountiful Sea

Although you might live thousands of miles from the nearest ocean, it has a great deal to do with your everyday life in many ways.

Its warm currents send heated air across mountains and valleys all over the world and this helps act as a regulator for our climate. Because of the ocean, ice and snow are kept away from many areas, which is one of the main reasons why farmers are able to grow their crops in soil that would otherwise be frozen. The ocean prevents the air from getting too dry, too hot or too cold.

Ocean waters not only supply the world with nutritious fish and shellfish, but they also produce a type of seaweed that is used by farmers for fertilizing many kinds of land crops. Certain seaweeds are used in the Orient as vegetables and in soup and Eskimos have included seaweed in their diet for many years. Irish moss, which grows on some kinds of rocks found on the New England coast, is made into a fine-tasting pudding.

Foods from the ocean may not taste as good as candy, but scientists think that, in the future, we will use even more produce from the shallows and depths of the salty seas than we do now. Experiments are being made to determine just how this can best be done, for in our fast-growing world, many people go hungry because fertile land is not plentiful.

Some scientists believe that the ocean could be used as a giant farm for, besides fish and shellfish, it contains a limitless supply of plankton, seaweed and many other kinds of edible food. If a way were discovered to cultivate, harvest and prepare these sea crops, just as earth farmers do with their crops, then probably enough food for everybody could be produced. This is, indeed, a challenge to anyone who wants to make worthwhile discoveries.

You might laugh at the idea of water farming, but it is already being done with oysters. In special locations, oyster shells are spread in shallow water and the baby oysters swimming around attach themselves to these shells. Slowly, they develop shells of their own and, while they grow into full-sized oysters, the sea farmer must tend his crops by keeping out starfish. If these marauders should get into the beds, they would kill and eat a great many oysters, which would ruin the farm.

Oceans all over the world are different in their ability to produce the food we take from them. In this respect, water is similar to land. In some places, where the soil and climate are just right, beautiful oranges or apples grow, while in other locations, such as dry deserts, hardly anything grows and little food is produced. In the barren places of the ocean, there are very few fish and shellfish, for animals of the sea stay where plankton and other food is abundant. But in the fertile places of the ocean, where there are acres and acres of drifting plankton, you will find enormous schools of fishes — and these places are like our fertile orchards. Some fishing areas have produced food for millions of people for many hundreds of years.

Perhaps the best known place in the world where a real ocean

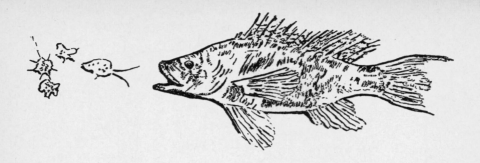

breadbasket exists, where there are enormous schools of codfish, is the Grand Banks, off Newfoundland — banks are relatively shallow places in the midst of the deep ocean. The warm Gulf Stream from the south and the cold Labrador Current from the north meet at the Grand Banks and an upwelling occurs so that the waters are very well mixed. The Labrador Current brings down minerals which fertilize the area and, as a result, there is a great deal of plankton — which supplies food to the tiniest of fish, and they in turn form the codfish's diet. Boats come from Europe and the United States to fish for cod on the Grand Banks. Millions of pounds of these fish are caught each year and are either salted down or frozen for world markets.

There are other banks besides those near Newfoundland that also produce great quantities of fish. Off the west coast of South America, where the cold Humboldt Current runs, many tons of herring are caught each year. Halibut are regularly taken in the cold waters off Alaska. Shrimp are plentiful in beds off the coast of Mexico. There are many other places, too, where good sea food can be caught for your dinner table by hard-working fishermen.

The ocean gives many things to many people. Iodine, which cures your cuts, first came from the sea, as does bromine, which is used in photography. From a certain seaweed, a jelly is made that helps scientists in their research to prevent disease. Many other drugs are also obtained from the sea.

It might come as a surprise to you to learn that one cubic mile of

sea water contains nearly twenty-five tons of silver. This is fifty thousand pounds! Unfortunately, at present, no one knows a cheap way to extract this, as well as the great amounts of gold and uranium that are in the sea. But other minerals are regularly mined from our oceans.

Salt is one product that we all use. Most of our table salt comes from mines on land but these mines got their rich supplies of salt millions of years ago when they were covered by the sea. Nowadays, in Europe, a great deal of salt is mined from the sea by allowing the water to flood shallow places on shore and then, after trapping it, waiting for the fresh water to evaporate, leaving sea salt behind.

Magnesium, a very important lightweight metal used in airplanes, can be extracted from the sea successfully.

The mineral potassium was first found in the burned ashes of a kind of seaweed called kelp.

The sea floor off such places as Venezuela and the Gulf Coast holds tremendous quantities of petroleum which oil companies regularly pump up and send to their refineries.

Even some jewelry comes from the sea. Pearls are found in oysters. Fish scales and shells are used for necklaces, earrings and bracelets. Some shells are even used as ash trays, dishes and horns. And shells have often been used as money by Indians in America, natives in Africa and in many other parts of the world.

The ocean also produces furs. The waters off the Aleutian Islands in the North Pacific are gathering places for sealers from several

Oil is pumped from the sea as well as from dry land.

countries, and if you see a nice fur coat made from the glossy hide of a seal, chances are it came from this region.

Many millions of years have passed since the oceans first formed in the creases and hollows of our earth, but it is only in recent years that certain secrets of the seas have become known. It is true that all the oceans of the world have been sailed on by now, but we still do not know everything about what makes up oceans, such as tides, currents, sea life, ocean bottom and so on. All these things grouped together form a science known as oceanography and many scientists throughout the world are spending their lives studying these secrets of the shallows and depths.

Oceans have always been important. All kinds of ships have carried soldiers to battlefields on many ocean routes; much of the wealth of the world has been gathered through trading across oceans; and continents and islands were settled by traveling over oceans. Truly, the ocean is the most important highway in the world. Even if you never go down into the ocean depths and make discoveries, it is exciting to read about them. And, by reading, you may not learn things that will help solve the mysteries of the ocean world, but you will certainly discover many wonderful facts for yourself.

Index

Polynesian natives, 74
Prince Henry, the Navigator, 72, 73
Puget Sound, 40

radar, 77, 78
radio, 77
Red Sea, 19, 22, 70
rivers (in the ocean), 26, 28, 29, 30
"roaring forties," 45
rock formation, 11

salt, 22, 24
sand, 65
"Santa Ana" wind, 46
Sargasso Sea, 30
seas, 19
sea water, 18
seaweed, 30, 89
Sea Wolf, 64
"seven seas," 19
ship's log, 76
Slocum, Joshua, 80
South Pacific, 13, 82
Spray, 80
spring tides, 34, 37
storms, 46, 47, 48, 51, 52, 53
Strait of Gibraltar, 41, 42, 66, 67, 70
Strait of Magellan, 74

straits, 36
submarines, 42, 63, 64, 65
sun, 10, 33, 34, 35, 36, 44
surf, 51

tidal currents, 36
tides, 32, 33, 34, 35, 36, 37
tide tables, 36, 37, 77
Titanic, 78
"trade winds," 46
treasure, 86, 87
"trenches," 57
trough (of wave), 50
Tsientang River, 37
typhoons, 46

United States, 28, 29, 30, 46, 72
upwelling, 40

Vikings, 72
volcanoes, 13, 14, 53, 54, 65

waterspout, 48
waves, 50, 51, 52, 53, 54
whirlpools, 38, 40
"Williwaw," 46
Wilm, 63
winds, 44, 45, 46, 47, 48, 51

Yellow Sea, 19